P9-BYA-249

SUPER SNIFFERS

DOG DETECTIVES ON THE JOB

Dorothy Hinshaw Patent

BLOOMSBURY
NEW YORK LONDON NEW DELHI SYDNEY

TABLE OF CONTENTS

1 DOGS AND THEIR AMAZING NOSES

Take a dog, any dog, for a walk along a sidewalk or in a park, and you won't be walking much—you'll be standing there holding a leash while the dog sniffs at every bush and every lamppost. While the dog sniffs, you're watching the scene around you, using your eyes to take in the world. Humans are visual creatures, while dogs "see" their world mostly through their highly sensitive noses.

Even though people and dogs experience the world very differently, they make perfect partners for one another. Wolves, which are ancestors of dogs, live in close family groups just like we do. So dogs are naturally adapted to live with us and to be our loyal companions.

Taffy spends most of her time on walks sniffing the ground to find out who else went this way.

Scientists have found that the wolf is the only ancestor to dogs, so even a miniature poodle is a wolf at heart.

Working Dogs Then and Now

Humans have taken advantage of dogs' superior sense of smell for thousands of years. Hunting dogs still find food, and herding dogs still use their noses to find wandering sheep, as they have for countless generations.

Since early in the twentieth century, people have discovered ways to put dogs' superior noses to new uses. During World War I, both sides used Red Cross dogs to locate wounded soldiers by scent and bring them medical aid. In World War II, dogs served as messengers, scouts, and guards on military bases. Their noses helped them find their way and recognize enemies. In Iraq and Afghanistan, dogs saved many lives by sniffing out buried explosive devices. Dogs are also used to make sure there are no hidden explosives in places where important people such as the US president will visit.

Now, in the twenty-first century, dogs have many new jobs that take advantage of their amazing sense of smell, sniffing out everything from bedbugs to illegal fruit—and lots more.

The US military can send a super-sniffing dog into just about any location by parachute.

Bedbugs are nasty pests that can hide in beds, curtains, furniture, luggage, and other places and bite people, causing itchy welts. Dogs such as Agent Q are able to sniff out bedbugs or their eggs tucked under a mattress or other location.

The Nose Knows

It's no wonder that a dog's snout sticks out, leading its way through the world. Not only does the muzzle put the dog's damp, curious nose up front, it also provides space for moist inner folds of tissue crammed with sensitive cells that can sort out thousands of odor messages in no time at all. Most scientists believe a human nose has somewhere between five and six million such nerve cells. That might sound like a lot, but a sheepdog's nose has more than two hundred million, and a bloodhound's nose has over three hundred million!

A dog has both more odor-sensitive cells than we do and a greater variety of cell types that take up far more surface area than ours. With this amazing sensitivity, dogs can detect countless aromas that the human nose doesn't even know are there. When a pizza order arrives at your house, you smell "pizza," or maybe "pepperoni pizza." Your dog smells each ingredient as a separate scent—tomato sauce, basil, onion, green pepper, cooked crust, wheat, mozzarella cheese, even the individual ingredients in the pepperoni.

Take a close look at a dog while it sniffs. Its moist nose quivers as it takes in puffs of fresh

Bloodhounds were bred to be the best scent searchers possible. When they are on trails, their long, floppy ears help stir up and funnel scent particles into their noses. The wrinkles on their faces also help direct scents.

air and blows out used air through the slits in the sides. The scent molecules in the air travel through the maze of nasal tissue, where the sensitive cells fire off messages telling the brain what's out there. A dog's brain is designed for scent, with forty times more brain area devoted to smell than in humans. No wonder dogs can help us with their noses.

Inside the snout of a dog are many folds of nasal tissue studded with millions and millions of cells that can detect odors too faint for humans to smell.

Some dogs are trained to search for one specific scent after sniffing a sample. Here, handler Bud Myers gives his bloodhound the scent of the person they will be seeking in this flooded North Dakota landscape.

Dogs Need Jobs

Humans have bred dogs for their ability and desire to be working partners. It's a good deal for both: the dog's needs for food and shelter are met, the human has help getting a job done, and each gets affection and companionship in return. Dog and human become a team of best buddies. A dog's job might be as simple as being a devoted companion to a loving person. But a true working dog wants a job that is a challenge to accomplish or a puzzle to solve. These are dogs that savor a reward, whether it's a food treat or a chance to play with a favorite toy.

Finding good candidates for scent work takes time. Some organizations visit animal shelters to find the right dogs. Other working dogs are bred especially for their jobs. Many organizations have their own breeding programs, which use volunteer families to raise the young dogs so they have a happy, healthy start in life. The puppies learn basic commands like "sit" and "stay" and are taken to all sorts of busy places so they get used to crowds and loud noises.

Military Working Dogs and their handlers become best friends who rely on one another to stay safe in dangerous places.

This Belgian Malinois (MAL-in-wah) puppy doesn't yet know that it will have an important job saving lives when it grows up.

Groups that provide dogs to help individual people, such as for diabetes alert work, look for dogs that are gentle, loyal, and strongly scent oriented. Dogs with searching jobs, such as explosives or missing-person finders, however, need to be energetic and intense, just the kinds of dogs that rarely make a good pet. These dogs need a job to satisfy their restless spirits.

Navy colonel Sam Kirby demonstrates how an explosive-device-detector dog is sent off to work.

Training an Expert Sniffer

The first step in a sniffer's training is to get the dog to realize it will be rewarded for recognizing a scent. The actual setup for training may vary, but the same basic steps are followed. Aldo and Linda Chwistek will demonstrate them for you on the next page.

Total training time for the first scent is usually six weeks to three months. These dogs are smart. Once they have learned how to find one scent, identifying a new one takes only a couple of weeks. The dogs learn quickly what the command "find it" means.

The dog uses a signal, called an alert, to indicate a find. An "active alert" is when the dog digs at the site of the find—such as bedbug finders, which scratch at the spot the bug scent comes from, or avalanche dogs, which dig in the snow covering a victim. Dogs whose job it is to locate explosives use a "passive alert," such as sitting or lying down next to the spot of the find.

Depending on its job, the dog gets either a food reward or a play reward, along with praise for a job well done. Dogs that work in the field, like Military Working Dogs (MWDs) or avalanche rescue dogs, work for a chance to play with their favorite toy. Dogs with indoor jobs, such as bedbug finders, usually receive food rewards. It isn't practical for a dog working in a home or hotel room to romp around playing with a toy!

This dog is learning to recognize the scent of bedbugs and has correctly chosen the container with the bugs inside.

MWDs are rewarded for finding explosives by getting to play with their favorite toy.

Step 1: Linda has put the target scent item and some food in an open container so that the odor can get out.

Step 2: That container is mixed in with others that have different target scents. Aldo searches the containers to find the scent.

Step 3: Linda rewards Aldo with food when he sniffs only at the container holding the target scent. Once he understands that finding the scent brings a reward, Linda repeats the process to reinforce the idea. Then the dog learns bit by bit how to find that odor on the job.

Challenges to Work

Sometimes, just getting to the job is hard work! The only way to get to most job sites in Afghanistan has been by helicopter.

Most scenting jobs require hard work, both for the dog and the handler. A dog that searches for missing persons may have to travel over large areas, often where there are limited roads or trails. MWDs that look for explosives have even greater challenges, since they are working in dangerous war zones.

Environmental conditions can affect a search. If it's very hot, a dog will have to pant to cool off, and it can't smell as well when it's panting. In wintertime, light, dry snow allows the scent to reach the surface more easily than does dense, wet snow. But during the rest of the year, moist air holds a scent much better than dry air. Wind can also affect a dog's ability to find a scent source. And since scent molecules are heavier than air, they can sink into low areas.

Despite the difficulties, with their sensitive noses dogs can find the desired odor quickly and with less expense than any man-made machine.

MWDs Ajax (left) and Jimmy (right) wear "doggles" on duty in Iraq to protect their eyes from sand that gets kicked up by helicopters and during sandstorms.

Megan Parker and conservation detection dog Wicket work in the heat, humidity, and steep terrain of Cameroon to find things that need protection, like endangered species, and things to get rid of, like weeds.

2 SEARCHING AND SAVING

Now that we've learned that our canine friends love to find things for us, we have begun using dogs to locate just about anything that has a scent, from gold ore and hidden money to gypsy moths and termites. You name it, a dog can find it!

The most common jobs for search dogs are finding people and finding explosives. Around the world, military units use dogs to find land mines, explosives in buildings, and the buried explosives on roads and trails known as "improvised explosive devices" (IEDs). These roadside bombs have killed many soldiers and civilians in Iraq and Afghanistan, and dogs are the most reliable way of locating them. Before a presidential visit, dogs check for explosive devices at the site. Dogs help make sure military bases are secure and also check for illegal drugs on base. After a natural disaster, dogs are brought in to search for victims, either living or dead. Because of their talent for finding things, search dogs are in demand around the world for these important jobs.

Dogs that search for people in disaster areas need to be able to climb over messy rubble with ease. By lying down, Rusty is telling his handler, Wayne Buford, that he can smell human scent here.

Officer James-Thiessen and Koko search a small plane that arrived into Canada.

Buddy and his handler, Army sergeant Tyler Barriere, demonstrate how they search for explosives.

Arson dog Callie is trained to recognize the scent of chemicals called accelerants, which are used by arsonists to help start fires.

Avalanche Rescue

When people are buried by an avalanche, searchers need to work fast to find them. While human rescuers can only walk around probing the snow with long poles in hopes of finding something, dogs move quickly, noses to the snow. The dogs can detect the human scent that works its way up through the snow to the surface from as deep as thirteen feet down. While a dog can find a victim in fifteen minutes and save his or her life, it could take days for a human search crew to find a body.

About 350 years ago, St. Bernards first began rescuing lost travelers in the Swiss Alps. After digging out a victim, one dog would lie on top of an injured person to keep him or her warm while another dog ran for help.

Otter, an avalanche dog, demonstrates how he tugs clothing from the snow to help rescue an avalanche victim.

If you watch Bode Calder playing tug-of-war with his canine buddy Otter, you'd think they were just having fun. But it's more than play—it's reinforcement of the vital skills Otter uses on the job with Bode's father, Joe. To train avalanche rescue dogs, their handlers get old wool sweaters from thrift shops, apply human scent, and bury them. The dogs learn to dig up the sweaters. Their reward is getting to play with the sweaters and tear them apart if they want to. This way, the dog learns to pull hard on any clothing it finds under the snow on a search.

Bode Calder uses a fun game to help train Otter.

Joe Calder and Otter spend most of the winter months demonstrating their training for guests at a Rocky Mountain ski resort and visiting injured skiers in the first-aid room. Still, they are always on call to rescue skiers should they be caught in an avalanche.

Finding Human Traces

Many different situations require the ability to find traces of human presence. To show respect for the dead, grave sites in old, forgotten cemeteries need to be precisely located. Crime scenes need to be safeguarded and explored. The remains of people lost in disasters need to be recovered.

A dog trained to find human traces must be able to recognize the scent of people who have died, even a long time ago. A search dog's sense of smell needs to be sensitive enough to detect everything from a single tooth to an entire body, even if it's buried deep in the ground. The dog also has to be able to work off leash and be willing to explore difficult and dangerous terrain, such as a building that has collapsed during an earthquake.

A search-and-rescue dog is carried up a ladder to look for victims in a building destroyed by an earthquake.

Legend, a Belgian Malinois, practices maneuvering over rubble piles to find traces of human remains.

Legend sniffs the ground for the odor of human remains at an old graveyard. She can even detect human traces that are nine hundred years old!

21

Military Working Dogs

Thousands of dogs perform important jobs for military forces around the world. Many of these dogs work on bases and in war zones, patrolling to check for illegal drugs, explosives, or intruders. In a war zone, MWDs are also trained to locate stashes of weapons and to follow the scent people have left after planting an explosive or committing a crime. These brave dogs not only help keep their handlers and other on-duty soldiers safe, but they also provide love and a sense of play in an often serious and scary environment.

The most intensely trained MWDs are called Specialized Search Dogs (SSDs). While some MWDs stay with a particular handler for one tour of duty, an SSD and its handler work together for as long as they both remain in service. These elite teams receive several months of training together. The dogs are trusted to work off leash in battle zones. The SSD teams focus on finding weapons, ammunition, and explosives, including the IEDs that can kill civilians as well as soldiers.

Australian Explosive Detection Dog Solo and his handler, Sapper Stuart Conlin, work at a checkpoint during an election in Afghanistan to make sure no vehicles containing explosives get through.

Super Sniffer
DEX

At first, Specialized Search trainee Marcin Radwan didn't think his dog-in-training, Dex, could possibly become his canine partner.

Dex was already a veteran SSD, but his previous handler had left the service. He didn't recognize Marcin as his handler, the person who would take care of him and tell him what to do. For example, Dex refused to give up his treasured toy on Marcin's command. But bit by bit, Marcin got Dex to trust that the toy would show up again. Dex kept wanting to be the boss, and Marcin kept showing that he, not the dog, was in command. Finally, after almost six months of desert training in Arizona, Dex began to trust Marcin and obey him without question.

In the war zone in Afghanistan, Dex worked well and enjoyed getting to sleep on the cot with his "dad" and to play every day—his work, sniffing out explosives, is play to him. He did his job well, helping to save soldiers from bombs. When they left the military, Marcin was able to adopt his canine pal. Now they can enjoy life together in a safe place.

Dex rests up after a hard day's work searching for explosives.

SSD Team Marcin Radwan and Dex search a building for explosives.

Marcin gives Dex a big hug for a job well done.

Law Enforcement Canines

This General Purpose Police Dog is helping to search a car in Great Britain for firearms, explosives, or drugs.

Dogs work around the world helping law enforcement officers do their jobs. They need to be strong and athletic so they can climb stairs, jump over walls, and chase criminals. They cannot be bothered by the many smells, noises, and bright lights of cities. They need to be brave and protective of their handlers in dangerous situations. All police dogs in the United States need to pass tests that show they are well trained, completely reliable, and obedient to their handlers.

Police dogs can have various jobs. The dogs know what work is expected of them by the equipment they wear and the commands they are given.

The dogs can search for explosives, much like MWDs do. Some are trained to recognize what's called a "vapor wake," the plume of odor emitted by explosives on the move. Dogs that can do this are useful in crowds, where a criminal might be carrying explosives in a backpack, ready to be set off.

Other dogs hunt for drugs. Dogs can use their noses instead of having to poke around and search under and inside things, getting the job done in a fraction of the time a person would take. Tracking suspected criminals and searching buildings are other jobs for police dogs.

Police dogs live with their human partners when they are off the job. However, the families must always remember that these dogs are serious working dogs. The dogs need to be well behaved and to always respond immediately to commands, even when playing and relaxing.

Handler Tim Harrington follows Halo as he tracks a human scent. Tim is wearing his SWAT team gear.

Ryker finds a stash of drugs in this container.

25

3 HELPING PLANET EARTH

As the world becomes more crowded with people, figuring out how to leave enough room for wild plants and animals becomes more difficult. Species are dying out at an increasing rate, and the natural world we depend on for our own survival is in danger. Around the planet, dogs are helping us by using their noses. They can sniff out both things we want to protect, such as endangered species, and things we want to get rid of, like weeds and polluted water.

Several organizations including Working Dogs for Conservation (WDC) in Montana and the University of Washington's Center for Conservation Biology have handled projects to protect and study endangered animals around the world, from tigers in Asia to lizards in California, jaguars in South America to wild dogs in Africa. Without disturbing the animals, dogs can help locate their poop, called "scat."

Tia and Alice Whitelaw, cofounder of WDC, keep track of San Joaquin kit foxes in California by locating their scat.

Wicket is rewarded with her ball after locating moon bear scat in China.

Tsavo, Wicket, and Tia take a break from looking for invasive brown tree snakes in Hawaii.

The scat provides scientists with a wealth of information—where the animals live, what they eat, how stressed they are, and even what their DNA reveals. Analyzing this information is vital to discovering the best way to help species in trouble. Conservation dogs can be trained to locate the scat of one particular species and ignore that of all others they encounter.

Invasive Weeds

As people travel more and more from one place to another, weed seeds can come with them on clothing and shoes, while the plants' natural enemies stay behind. Without diseases and predators to control them, these weeds overrun the local species. This can make it hard for native animals to find the food they need, and can turn a hillside that once supported dozens of plant species into a single-species carpet.

Europeans imported a plant called dyer's woad from central Asia in ancient times for the beautiful blue dye they could extract from its leaves, and then brought it with them to America. Now it has become an invasive weed that quickly spreads and crowds out native plants, especially in the western states. For fourteen years, human workers have tried to get rid of dyer's woad with little success, because the young sprouts are hard to see among native vegetation.

WDC trains dogs to nose out dyer's woad plants in Montana. Intense, active Seamus (right) can find even the tiniest young plant barely peeking up out of the ground so it can be removed before it has a chance to go to seed.

The long, deep root of dyer's woad makes it especially hard to get rid of the plant.

Weed-hunting dogs have been so successful that sometimes there are no new plants to find. When that happens, a handler leaves one or two young plants in place to make sure the dog will always get a reward when it works.

When he locates a weed plant, Seamus wags his tail and lies down with the find between his front legs.

After a successful find, Seamus's handler, Dalit Guscio, gives him his favorite ball and praises him for doing a good job.

29

Vanishing Gorillas

The Cross River gorilla subspecies is so rare that scientists thought it was extinct until the 1980s when there were new sightings. Gorillas reproduce slowly. A female is likely to give birth to only three or four surviving young in her lifetime. And with fewer than three hundred individuals left, the Cross River gorilla is the most critically endangered of all. Conservationists hope that by using dogs to locate gorilla scat, called dung, they can determine where the gorillas spend time and also study the relationships among individuals. Both Nigeria and Cameroon have set aside national parks to protect the gorillas and other wildlife, but until now, little has been known about the distribution and habitat of these apes. Conservationists are in a race against time, as human activities such as logging and hunting divide up the gorillas' habitat and reduce their numbers.

The Cross River subspecies of gorilla is highly endangered.

Super Sniffer
LILY

Labrador retriever mix Lily had a problem: people didn't know what to do with such an intense and active dog. After five failed adoptions, Lily ended up at a Georgia animal shelter. Realizing that Lily needed a job, the shelter sent her to WDC in Montana. Since then, Lily has happily pursued a number of scents, from grizzly bear scat in Alaska to the smell of an insect called the emerald ash borer that kills trees in Minnesota. She's even learning how to find wire traps used by poachers in Africa to catch game illegally. When a trap is found, it can be removed to make life safer for animals.

One of Lily's biggest adventures was traveling to the country of Cameroon, in Africa, to locate the scat of the rare Cross River gorilla. Along with two other WDC dogs, she bounced along rutted country roads in the back of a truck to reach the remote forest where these secretive apes live. The dogs and their handlers worked their way though dense rain forest and up and down steep slopes in search of gorilla dung. Lily's high energy and sharp focus on her job made her perfect for this challenging task.

Lily happily hunts for the dung of the Cross River gorilla in Cameroon.

Lily has made a find! You can see the dung over to the right in the photo.

Endangered Orcas

Scientists have studied the powerful orcas that live along the coast of Washington State for decades. They know when each was born, who its mother is, where the whales live at different times of the year, and other details about their lives. Each individual orca has a unique pattern of black-and-white markings, making it easily recognizable. The whales' scat contains DNA that can also identify individuals.

Tourists come from all over the world to see the whales, and conservationists and scientists alike have been concerned about the effects whale-watching boats, declines in fish populations, and waterborne toxins might be having on the orcas. The orca population has been dwindling in recent years, and scientists want to learn whether the noisy boats stress the whales or if there are other reasons for the population decline. If they can find out what stresses the orcas, they can direct wildlife policies to help the whales.

Whale scat can reveal much about the lives of the orcas. Through the DNA in the scat, scientists can figure out which whale the scat came from and what prey that whale has been eating. Scat also contains traces of stress hormones and hormones associated with nutrition.

Tucker, a former stray, has become an expert at recognizing the scat of orcas before it sinks down into the sea around the San Juan Islands in Washington State.

Thanks to Tucker, the scientists have been able to collect whale scat, analyze it, and compare all that information with data on salmon populations

This whale-watching boat is close to an orca, but the whale doesn't seem to be bothered.

and the activity of tour boats. They found that stress hormones in the scat were at their lowest in August, when salmon were abundant and lots of whale-watching boats were around. But in late September, when both the salmon and tour boats decreased, stress hormones went up. Now they know that the tour boats don't affect the whales much as long as they have plenty of salmon.

Tucker sneaks a kiss at his handler, Elizabeth Seely.

When Tucker catches the scent of scat, he leans over the bow, letting his handler know when to turn the boat to scoop up the sample. Tucker's amazing nose can locate even a tiny speck of orca scat more than a mile away.

Contaminated Water

Water is our most precious resource. It's important not only for the natural environment but also for our very survival. When raw sewage gets into the water system, it causes many problems, such as fueling overgrown algae that steals oxygen from fish, making our drinking water unsafe, and contaminating the water we swim in.

When water enters a storm drain or when you flush a toilet, the water goes into pipes that travel underground for miles before reaching a sewage plant for treatment to make the water safe.

Riff is being trained to recognize human sewage. He lies down to show his handler, Celeste Thomas, that he's found the sample.

Scott Reynolds and Sable look for evidence of sewage in a creek in West Virginia.

Sometimes raw sewage leaks from those pipes into the pipes carrying fresh rainwater to rivers, lakes, and oceans, causing contamination.

Pinpointing where contamination was entering drain systems used to waste precious time, until the idea of using dogs' noses to solve the problem was introduced. Laboratory tests can take days to get answers, but a dog's nose can sense telltale traces of sewage right away.

Super Sniffer

LOGAN

Logan had a tough start in life. His first family had lost their beloved collie and got Logan to replace her. But Logan wasn't calm like their first dog. Even Karen Reynolds, the trainer the family hired to work with him, found him a challenge. Then one day, his people tried to take away a bone Logan was chewing on and he snapped at them. They decided he was a vicious dog that needed to be put down, but Karen knew better. She realized that dogs can be very possessive about bones, and that snapping when someone tried to take a bone away didn't mean that Logan would really bite. She couldn't bear to see this highly intelligent, energetic dog put down, so she made him part of her own family.

Because of Karen's other job, she also realized that Logan's energy and possessiveness could be put to good use. Karen and her husband, Scott, own Environmental Canine Services (ECS), and they trained Logan as an "illicit discharge detection" dog. That means Logan can detect the smallest trace of sewage in water. For example, when beaches on the shores of the Great Lakes in Michigan had to be closed, Logan helped trace the sources of the sewage that had contaminated the storm runoff entering the lakes.

Before ECS came along, people had to take water samples to a laboratory for analysis, which might take days. But Logan can find sewage in the water immediately, saving money and helping to end the contamination much sooner.

Logan and his handler, Karen, are best buddies.

Logan indicates he's found human sewage in the water and looks up expectantly to Karen for his reward.

4 MEDICAL ALERT DOGS

In recent years, people began to notice that dogs could detect human medical problems. Now dogs have become important helpers in modern medicine. Because of their amazing noses, they can sense chemical changes in a person's body that indicate dangerous chemical imbalances or the presence of disease. They can also recognize allergens, substances that cause allergic reactions in some people.

Even though scientists often don't know exactly how a dog is being alerted to a medical problem, they know that it works. Dogs can free people from worries about their medical issues. They can detect the presence of certain kinds of cancer in samples of urine or in a person's breath. In the future, scientists will likely find even more ways a dog's keen nose can help improve modern medicine.

Nano is learning how to detect traces of both peanuts and nuts that grow on trees to protect her owner, Yasmin Tomblad, from serious allergic reactions.

Daisy can identify the odor of cancer in the sample that's underneath the metal paddle.

A boy with diabetes checks his blood sugar level while his diabetes alert dog snuggles up.

37

Monitoring Addison's Disease

Medical Detection Dogs, a charity in the United Kingdom, specializes in training dogs to help people with life-threatening conditions by alerting them when they need help. We now know dogs can sniff out a variety of imbalances in the body caused by a lack of vital chemicals called hormones.

For example, cortisone and other hormones made by the adrenal glands are involved in essential body processes. In a rare disorder called Addison's disease, the adrenal glands don't produce enough of these hormones, which can cause a variety of dangerous symptoms such as severe pain, vomiting, confusion, convulsions, loss of consciousness, or a life-threatening drop in blood pressure.

Karen has Addison's disease, and sometimes she would end up in the hospital because she couldn't recognize when she needed cortisone until she was dangerously ill. She felt trapped in her home. Coco is trained to recognize when her cortisone is low. With Coco at her side, Karen can now lead a normal life, confident that Coco will let her know when she needs more life-saving cortisone.

Karen and Coco participate in a parade to show people how an alert dog can help people with medical problems live normal lives.

While Karen enjoys watching a tennis match at Wimbledon, Coco stays on guard and will let Karen know if she needs to give herself a shot.

When Karen's cortisone levels get too low, Coco will alert her and even bring her a bag containing the cortisone and syringe she needs.

Controlling Diabetes

Diabetes is a very common disease that affects millions of people of all ages. Normally, a hormone called insulin controls the level of sugar in the bloodstream and gets the energy-rich sugar to the cells in the body so that they can work properly.

In diabetes, the relationship between insulin, sugar, and the body doesn't work right, and people with the disease sometimes need to be given insulin to help solve the problem. Some people get diabetes when they are children. For some reason, their bodies destroy the cells in an organ called the pancreas, where insulin is made. When this happens, the cells in their bodies don't get the energy they need from sugar to function normally. This is called Type 1 diabetes.

Several organizations in the United States and other countries train dogs to recognize problems with insulin. Some of these dogs are trained to alert people to both high blood sugar, when the person needs more insulin, and low blood sugar, when the person needs to eat a sugary snack. In order to train a dog for this job, the dog is presented with a scraping of skin from a person whose blood sugar is low. The dog learns to recognize the way skin smells at that time and to alert the person to that odor. They can also be trained to recognize the odor brought about by high blood sugar.

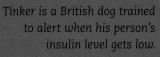

Tinker is a British dog trained to alert when his person's insulin level gets low.

Super Sniffer OAKLEY

Oakley was originally being trained to be a service dog for a person with a disability. That job didn't work out, because Oakley was a bit too shy. Instead, she went to Early Alert Canines, an organization that trains dogs to help people with diabetes. There, she became a skilled companion dog for Nathan, who has Type 1 diabetes. Because Nathan's body doesn't make insulin, he gets daily injections of it, as well as an extra shot when he eats food that has a lot of carbohydrates. But sometimes the insulin does too good a job, and Nathan's blood sugar gets dangerously low. When that happens, Oakley finds Nathan's mom and lets her know her son needs a sugary snack. As her reward, Oakley gets her favorite treat, a cheese stick.

At the end of the day, Oakley sleeps in Nathan's room in case his blood sugar drops during the night. If that happens, she will alert his parents. Oakley is always on the job, even while the family is sleeping.

Oakley is constantly on the job to keep Nathan safe. She wears a scarf to show that she's working.

Oakley isn't just a working dog, she's a member of Nathan's family.

Cancer Finders

A few years ago, people began to report that they had been alerted to having cancer by their dogs. For example, one dog kept nosing a dark spot on her owner's leg, which turned out to be a dangerous cancer called melanoma. Doctors began to wonder—do cancers have unusual odors that dogs can detect?

Since then, scientists in Great Britain, Germany, and the United States have been studying this idea. They found that, yes, dogs *can* sense the presence of at least some cancers, and have been training them to do so. The dogs don't actually sniff at the person—they have learned to recognize certain cancers in samples of the person's breath or urine. They are given a choice of samples from a variety of people and can pick out the one from someone with cancer.

Stewie can smell which of these containers has a sample inside from a person with breast cancer.

Stewie is allowed to go into stores because she's a service dog.

Stewie and her person, Dina Zaphiris Garbis, are pioneers in the new medical world of cancer detection by odor. Stewie and Dina work with the InSitu Foundation, which trains dogs to detect cancer in humans at its earliest stages, when it is most treatable. Over time, the foundation hopes to create a screening process with the help of dogs like Stewie so that people can get the early cancer treatment that often leads to a cure.

Stewie and her buddy, Katie, love going to the beach and playing in the water when they're not working.

Puppies are being trained to detect ovarian cancer by Cynthia Otto, DVM, PhD, as part of a cooperative University of Pennsylvania and Monell Chemical Senses Center program.

Allergy Alert Dogs

No one knows why, but food allergies among children have been increasing. Children can react to a variety of foods, including eggs, dairy products, and spices. Peanut allergies are especially common, creating a serious problem in a world where peanuts are a popular snack and food ingredient.

Some children have life-threatening allergies to even the smallest trace of an allergen and can end up in the hospital with difficulty breathing, as well as other nasty symptoms such as severe itching. Luckily, dogs, with their incredible ability to sniff out the tiniest bit of an allergy-producing substance, are being used to protect these children and help give them more normal lives. Like medical alert dogs, allergy alert dogs go everywhere with the people so they can provide constant protection.

Goldendoodle LilyBelle places her paw on a jar containing nuts—an ability that helps her warn seven-year-old Meghan Weingarth to stay away.

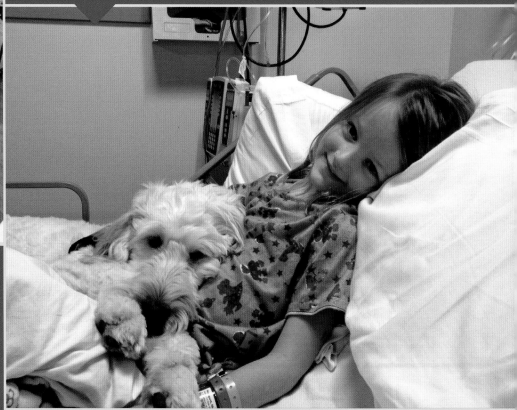

LilyBelle goes everywhere with Meghan and comforts her when she is in the hospital.

Super Sniffer
DECLAN

Declan is a natural sniffer. Here he checks out a slide for traces of peanut scent.

No one had any idea what lay ahead for the small black stray with an injured leg when he arrived at the BARC Shelter in Baltimore in 2012. He found a temporary home with Michelle Northam and her friend Aaron Kirkpatrick, who nursed him back to health and named him Radar, for his oversized ears. Meanwhile, Nikhi Cormier, up north in Nova Scotia, worried about her daughter, Lo, whose severe peanut allergy often sent her to the hospital. Nikhi came across the fan page for my book *Saving Audie*, about an energetic and smart little pit bull who became a champion scent competition dog. Could such a dog help Lo?

Nikhi found big-eared Radar online and fell in love with him, adopted him, and renamed him Declan, meaning "full of goodness." Declan is training at Tecla's K-9 Academy in Maryland for his important job. His nose can detect the tiniest whiff of peanuts up close. If someone holds a nut and then touches a computer key, Declan can pick up the scent. Once he learns to be comfortable in all sorts of environments, from noisy malls to smelly buses, and can sniff out a peanut from three feet away, Declan will be united with Lo. With Declan by her side, Lo will be able to live a safe and nearly normal life.

Lo enjoys looking for fossils in a quarry with her grandmother's dog, Griffin, while she waits for Declan to join the family.

Declan takes a break from training.

Further Reading and Surfing

Books for Young Readers

Carney, Elizabeth. *Dog Finds Lost Dolphins!: And More True Stories of Amazing Animal Heroes*. Washington, DC: National Geographic, 2012.

Profiles of animal heroes, including a dog who used his nose to find stranded dolphins.

Castaldo, Nancy F. *Sniffer Dogs: How Dogs (and Their Noses) Save the World*. New York: HMH Books for Young Readers, 2014.

Information about various kinds of scenting dogs and how they help people.

Jackson, Donna M. *Hero Dogs: Courageous Canines in Action*. New York: Little, Brown Books for Young Readers, 2003.

True stories of amazing dog rescuers.

Patent, Dorothy Hinshaw. *Dogs on Duty: Soldiers' Best Friends on the Battlefield and Beyond*. New York: Walker Books for Young Readers, 2012.

How dogs have been and still are helping to protect and save members of the military forces using their sense of smell.

Ring, Elizabeth. *Detector Dogs: Hot on the Scent*. Minneapolis: The Millbrook Press, 1993.

Examines the many ways dogs use their keen sense of smell to help law enforcement personnel in all kinds of detective work.

Websites

Searching and Saving

www.searchdogfoundation.org
An organization that trains search-and-rescue dogs, with links to videos and further information

www.gpsar.org/hugatree.html
This site describes the Hug-a-Tree program, which helps children learn what to do if they get lost in the woods. Search-and-rescue dogs are often used to help find lost children.

Helping Planet Earth

http://conservationbiology.uw.edu/conservation-canines
Information about the organization that Tucker and other conservation dogs work with

http://workingdogsforconservation.org
An organization that uses trained dogs to detect invasive weeds, endangered species, and pests

Medical Alert Dogs

www.earlyalertcanines.org
A website for diabetes alert dogs

www.medicaldetectiondogs.org.uk
An organization in the United Kingdom that pioneers medical detection work and trains dogs for various detection jobs

Acknowledgments and Photo Credits

To the memory of my dearest canine friends: Ricky, Buffy, Lena, Elsa, and Ninja—Super Sniffers all!

Most of my research for this book involved finding organizations and individuals that are involved in the various kinds of work these amazing dogs do for us, studying their websites, and interviewing the experts. I'm especially grateful to the folks at Conservation Canines, Early Alert Canines, Medical Detection Dogs, and Working Dogs for Conservation for their assistance. I found that the people who work with the dogs are all wonderfully enthusiastic and helpful—the Anderson family, Joe Calder, Nikhi Cormier, John Donges, Carol Edwards, Dina Zaphiris Garbis, Tim Harrington, Mike Kamerer, Bev Peabody, Sgt. Marcin Radwan, Scott and Karen Reynolds, and Ken Rider. Thanks also to Linda Chwistek, Bill Cook, Cammie Hinshaw, and Nancy Schiesari for their help with the project.

I also read various articles and scientific papers in magazines and newspapers dealing with canine scenting abilities, including: Kenneth G. Furton and Lawrence J. Myers, "The Scientific Foundation and Efficacy of the Use of Canines as Chemical Detectors for Explosives," *Talanta* 54, no. 3 (May 10, 2001): 487–500; and Margie Pfiester, Philip G. Koehler, and Roberto M. Pereira, "Ability of Bed Bug–Detecting Canines to Locate Live Bed Bugs and Viable Bed Bug Eggs," *Journal of Economic Entomology* 101, no. 4 (August 2008): 1389–96.

Copyright © 2014 by Dorothy Hinshaw Patent

All rights reserved. No part of this book may be reproduced or transmitted in any form or by any means, electronic or mechanical, including photocopying, recording, or by any information storage and retrieval system, without permission in writing from the publisher.

First published in the United States of America in September 2014
by Bloomsbury Children's Books
www.bloomsbury.com

Bloomsbury is a registered trademark of Bloomsbury Publishing Plc

For information about permission to reproduce selections from this book, write to Permissions, Bloomsbury Children's Books,
1385 Broadway, New York, New York 10018

Bloomsbury books may be purchased for business or promotional use. For information on bulk purchases please contact Macmillan Corporate and Premium Sales Department at specialmarkets@macmillan.com

Library of Congress Cataloging-in-Publication Data
available upon request
ISBN 978-0-8027-3618-5

Typeset in Caecilia LT Std • Book design by Amanda Bartlett
Printed in China by Leo Paper Products, Heshan, Guangdong
1 3 5 7 9 10 8 6 4 2

All papers used by Bloomsbury Publishing, Inc., are natural, recyclable products made from wood grown in well-managed forests. The manufacturing processes conform to the environmental regulations of the country of origin.

Photo Credits

Courtesy of the Anderson family: 41 (both); the Canadian Border Services Agency: 17 (right top); Caters News Agency: 44 (both); Center for Conservation Biology: 33 (top, Julia Marks; bottom, Jane Cogan); Bill Cook: 13 (all); Nikhi Cormier: 45 (middle); Robert Domm: 35 (right); John Donges: 43 (bottom); Environmental Canine Services: 34 (both), 35 (left); FEMA: 16, 20; Getty Images: 1, 8, 37 (left); Donna Gladstone-Szymanski: 45 (top and bottom); Grand Targhee Resort: 3, 18 (right), 19 (left); iStockphoto: 9 (top); Medical Detection Dogs: 36, 37 (right), 38, 39 (both); Dorothy Hinshaw Patent: 4, 19 (right), 25 (both), 28, 29 (both); Bev Peabody, 21 (both); Marcin Radwan: 23 (all); Garrett Ryan: 42 (left), 43 (top); David Trietiak, K9 P.I.: 7; UK Ministry of Defence: 24; US Department of Defense: 2, 6, 10, 11 (both), 12 (bottom), 14, 15 (right), 17 (left), 22; Victorian Picture Library: 18 (left); Wikimedia: 5, 9 (bottom), 12 (top), 17 (right bottom), 30 (Julie Langford), 32 (Kirstin Poulsen), 40; Working Dogs for Conservation: 15 (left), 26, 27 (both), 31 (both); Dina Zaphiris: 42 (right)

Index

Note: *Italic* page numbers indicate photographs.